Serving Your Country

The Canadian Forces Snowbirds:

431 Air Demonstration Squadron

by Lora Polack Oberle

Consultant:
Captain Eric Pootmans
Utility Pilot–Snowbird 13
431 Air Demonstration Squadron–Snowbirds

CAPSTONE
HIGH-INTEREST
BOOKS

an imprint of Capstone Press

Capstone High-Interest Books are published by Capstone Press
151 Good Counsel Drive, P.O. Box 669, Mankato, Minnesota 56002
http://www.capstone-press.com

Library of Congress Cataloging-in-Publication Data
Oberle, Lora Polack.
  The Canadian Forces Snowbirds: 431 Air Demonstration Squadron/by Lora
Polack Oberle.
    p. cm.—(Serving your country)
    Includes bibliographical references and index.
    ISBN 0-7368-0774-8
    1. Canada. Canadian Armed Forces. Snowbirds—Juvenile literature. 2. Stunt
flying—Canada—Juvenile literature. [1. Canada. Canadian Armed Forces.
Snowbirds. 2. Stunt flying.] I. Title. II. Series.
UG635.C2 O25 2001
797.5'4'0971—dc21   00-009952

Summary: Describes the Canadian Forces Snowbirds, their history, aircraft,
maneuvers, and team members.

Editorial Credits
Carrie A. Braulick, editor; Lois Wallentine, product planning editor; Timothy
    Halldin, cover designer; Linda Clavel, production designer and illustrator;
    Katy Kudela, photo researcher

Photo Credits
DND Photo, 10, 13, 14
Garry Cotter, 42
Gayln C. Hammond, 27, 30, 39
John Alves/Mystic Wanderer Images, 40
Katsuhiko Tokunaga, 20
Paul MacGregor, 37
Rafe Tomsett, cover
Russ Heinl, 4, 6, 28, 32, 34
Unicorn Stock Photos/MacDonald Photography, 16; Rod Furgason, 18

1 2 3 4 5 6 06 05 04 03 02 01

Table of Contents

Chapter 1
The Canadian Forces Snowbirds

The nine red, white, and blue planes fly above
the crowd at the air show. They roll and loop as
one unit. They form various shapes such as an
arrow and a heart. Some of the planes fly upside
down. A skilled team of Canadian military pilots
flies these planes. This team is known as
the Snowbirds.

Flight Demonstration
The Snowbirds' official name is 431 Air
Demonstration Squadron. The team is part of the

The Snowbirds fly nine planes during air shows.

The Snowbirds fly red, white, and blue CT-114 Tutors.

Canadian Forces. The Snowbird pilots
serve in the Canadian Air Force.

The Snowbirds perform aerobatic
maneuvers such as loops and rolls with their
planes. They also fly in close formation.

Each show season, the Snowbirds fly in
about 75 air shows at 50 different North
American locations. The Snowbirds' show

season runs from May through October each year.

The Snowbirds have flown in more than 1,700 air shows since the team formed in 1971. More than 100 million people have watched them fly. In the United States, the Snowbirds have performed at Fourth of July celebrations. They also performed at Walt Disney World's 20th anniversary celebration. The Snowbirds have performed at anniversary celebrations for Canada and for the Canadian Air Force.

The Snowbirds are one of the world's largest plane demonstration teams. Nine pilots perform during air shows. Only the British, Polish, and Italian plane demonstration teams fly as many planes.

The CT-114 Tutor

The Snowbirds' plane is the CT-114 Tutor. The Tutor has a jet engine. This engine burns fuel to create exhaust gases. The exhaust gases shoot out the rear of the plane. The plane then

Snowbirds' Emblem

moves forward. A plane with a jet engine often is called a "jet."

The Tutor is 32 feet (9.8 meters) long. It has a wingspan of 36 feet (11 meters). It stands about 9 feet (3 meters) high. The Tutor's top speed is about 470 miles (760 kilometers) per hour.

Tutors are ideal for demonstration flying. They are smaller and slower than many other military planes. The planes' design allows the Snowbirds to fly in large formations while keeping the show in front of the audience.

The Snowbirds' Tutors are decorated. They are painted red and white. These are Canada's official colors. The planes also have a blue stripe on their sides. Part of the Snowbirds' emblem is painted in white on the bottom of the planes. This symbol represents the Snowbirds.

The Snowbirds' Tutors are stationed at 15 Wing. This military base is located south of the city of Moose Jaw, Saskatchewan, Canada. The Snowbird pilots train at the base. Beginning Canadian Air Force pilots also learn to fly at 15 Wing.

Chapter 2
Snowbirds' History

The Snowbirds are an important part of the Canadian Forces' history. They have existed longer than any of the Canadian Forces' previous flight demonstration teams. But these earlier demonstration teams were important to the organization of the Snowbirds.

The Siskins

The first Canadian Forces' flight demonstration team was called the Siskins. Three pilots formed this team in 1929. They flew Armstrong-Whitworth Siskin IIIA biplanes. Biplanes have two sets of wings.

The Golden Hawks performed in air shows from 1959 to 1963.

The Siskin IIIAs were among the best fighter planes during the 1920s. Fighter planes are designed to shoot down enemy planes.

The Siskins performed for three years. They flew more than 100 demonstrations.

The Golden Hawks

In 1959, the Royal Canadian Air Force (RCAF) celebrated its 35th anniversary. The RCAF was the name of the Canadian Air Force before 1968. The RCAF formed a flight demonstration team called the Golden Hawks to publicize the event. The Golden Hawks included six pilots. These pilots flew in close formation. Two solos sometimes performed routines separate from the formations. The Golden Hawks later added a seventh pilot to the team.

The Golden Hawks flew gold and red F-86 Sabre planes. Many of the world's militaries used these fighter planes during the 1950s. A large red and white hawk was painted on each side of the planes.

The Golden Hawks flew more than 300 demonstrations in five years. But supporting

The Siskins flew three Siskin IIIA biplanes in formation.

the team was expensive for the RCAF. The Golden Hawks disbanded in 1963.

The Golden Centennaires

In 1967, Canada celebrated its 100th anniversary. The RCAF formed a new demonstration team. It was called the Golden Centennaires.

The Golden Centennaires flew nine CT-114 Tutors in formation. The Centennaires' Tutors were painted gold and blue.

The Golden Centennaires performed for one year. They flew in more than 100 North American air shows. More than 15 million people saw them fly.

The Snowbirds Form

In 1970, Colonel Owen Philp was commander of 15 Wing. He also had been commander of the Golden Centennaires. Philp noticed several of the Centennaires' old Tutors at the base. He believed that demonstration flying was important. Philp decided to start a new flight demonstration team with the Tutors.

Philp asked instructor pilots at the base to volunteer for the new team. Seven instructors agreed to join the team. These pilots began to practice during their spare time. The pilots performed on weekends. They flew only in close formation. They did not perform aerobatic maneuvers.

The pilots held a contest for students at the base's elementary school to name their new team. Doug Farmer suggested the name "Snowbirds" and won the contest.

Owen Philp formed the Snowbirds in 1970.

The Snowbirds fly in a variety of formations.

On July 11, 1971, the team flew its
first demonstration as the Snowbirds.
This performance was at the Saskatchewan
Homecoming Air Show. The Snowbirds also
performed at several other air shows
throughout the year.

Many changes for the Snowbirds occurred
throughout the 1970s. In 1972, the Snowbirds
added two solos. In 1973, the team started to
perform aerobatic maneuvers. On April 1,

1978, the Snowbirds received full squadron status. They become an official squadron in the Canadian Forces. The Snowbirds received the name 431 Air Demonstration Squadron at this time.

Team Highlights

On May 11, 1975, the Snowbirds became the first North American flight demonstration team to perform in the Arctic. This region surrounds the North Pole. The Arctic includes many islands and the northern parts of Asia, Europe, and North America.

In 1988, the Snowbirds performed at the Winter Olympic Games in Calgary, Alberta, Canada. Millions of people worldwide watched the team's performance on TV.

In 1993, the Snowbirds flew their first performance outside of Canada and the United States. They performed at three air shows in Guadalajara, Mexico.

In 1999, the Snowbirds celebrated 25 years of service in the Canadian Forces. The Canadian Forces presented a decorative flag called the Squadron Standard to the team.

Chapter 3
Aircraft and Maneuvers

The Snowbirds perform about 50 different maneuvers during each show. Pilots allow no more than 10 seconds between the maneuvers. This sequence helps keep the show interesting for audiences. A Snowbird performance lasts about 35 minutes.

The Tutor's History

Canadair designed the Tutor in the late 1950s. This aircraft manufacturing company is located in Montreal, Quebec, Canada. The Tutor was first called the CL41-A. In January 1960, a

The Snowbirds perform about 50 different maneuvers during each show.

The Snowbirds' Tutors are modified to help the pilots perform aerobatic maneuvers.

pilot flew a CL41-A model for the first time. In 1961, the RCAF agreed to purchase 190 CL41-As from Canadair. The RCAF then renamed these planes CT-114 Tutors.

In 1973, the Tutor became the Canadian Forces' advanced jet trainer. Two side-by-side seats are in the cockpit. Both the instructor and student can operate the plane's controls.

The Snowbirds' Tutors

The Snowbirds' Tutors are similar to the training Tutors. But the Snowbirds' planes are modified to allow the pilots to fly solo from either seat. The Snowbirds' Tutors have radio equipment that allows the pilots to talk to each other before they start the planes' engines. This equipment allows the Snowbirds to start performing together as a show begins. Radio equipment in other Tutors only allows pilots to talk to each other after the engines are running. The steering in the Snowbirds' Tutors also is adjusted to allow the pilots to make sharper turns when they taxi. Pilots travel along the runway when they taxi.

Each of the Snowbirds' Tutors has a smoke generating system. This system creates white smoke. Two tanks are attached to the plane's bottom. Each tank contains about 35 gallons (130 liters) of diesel fuel. The pilots push a trigger in the cockpit. Fuel then comes out of the tanks and sprays into the plane's exhaust. The mixture of fuel and exhaust produces the white smoke.

The Snowbirds fly 11 Tutors to air shows. They use the two extra planes in demonstrations if planes break down.

The Big Diamond

The basic Snowbird formation is called the Big Diamond. All nine planes fly in a diamond shape during this formation. The pilots have numbers that relate to their positions in the Big Diamond.

Snowbird No. 1 is called the team lead or "boss." The boss leads the Big Diamond and the other Snowbird formations. The boss also calls all formation changes and maneuvers to other pilots on a radio. The commands allow pilots to smoothly change from one maneuver to the next.

The Big Diamond has eight other positions. Snowbirds No. 2 and No. 3 fly on the left and right sides of the boss. They are called the inner wingers or "inners." Snowbirds No. 4 and No. 5 fly directly behind the boss. They are the first and second line asterns. These pilots make up the formation's "stem." Snowbirds No. 6 and No. 7 fly behind and to the left and right of Snowbird No. 4. They are called the outer wingers or "outers." Snowbirds No. 8 and No. 9

The Big Diamond

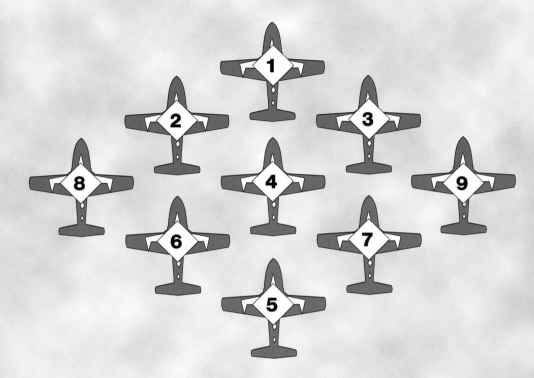

Snowbird #1	**Team lead**
Snowbird #2	**Inner right winger**
Snowbird #3	**Inner left winger**
Snowbird #4	**First line astern**
Snowbird #5	**Second line astern**
Snowbird #6	**Outer right winger**
Snowbird #7	**Outer left winger**
Snowbird #8	**Lead solo**
Snowbird #9	**Opposing solo**

Snowbird Formations

Palm

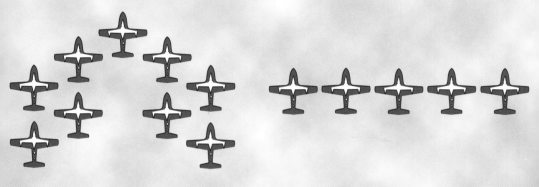

Line Abreast

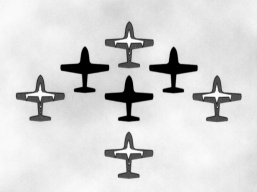

Double Diamond

Inverted Split

<table>
<tr><td>✈ Inverted planes</td></tr>
</table>

fly on the far left and right sides of the Big Diamond. These two pilots are the "solos." One of these pilots is the lead solo. This pilot gives commands for solo maneuvers. The other pilot is the opposing solo.

Maneuvers and Aerobatics
Snowbird pilots perform difficult maneuvers. They must be precise during flight. They often perform maneuvers in close formation. The planes sometimes are less than 4 feet (1.2 meters) apart. A mistake could cause the planes to touch and crash.

The Line Abreast Roll to Loop is one of the Snowbirds' most challenging maneuvers. During this maneuver, five pilots fly their aircraft side-by-side in the Line Abreast formation. They perform loops and rolls while they remain in line. These maneuvers are difficult because the planes are only about 8 feet (2.4 meters) apart.

Seven planes perform the Inverted Split Pass maneuver. The planes form the shape of a stemmed arrow to make the Inverted Split formation. The inners and first line astern turn upside down. The boss then flies in a different direction to allow the crowd to see the inverted planes clearly.

During the Downward Burst, nine pilots fly in the Palm formation. Four planes fly on each side of the boss during this formation. The pilots perform a combination of a roll and a loop called a cloverleaf. As the pilots fly toward the ground, they break away from the formation.

During the Double Diamond Roll, seven planes fly in the Double Diamond formation. In this formation, three planes fly nose to tail. Two planes then fly on each side of the three planes. They perform a roll as they pass in front of the audience. The planes are closer together in this maneuver than in any of the others. The wingtips overlap one another by as much as 8 feet (2.4 meters).

During the Lag Back Cross, three pilots closely cross paths. It appears that they fly

The Snowbirds sometimes fly in the Double Diamond formation.

through one another. But the planes are about 33 feet (10 meters) apart as they cross.

The Snowbirds sometimes take off and land in the Big Diamond formation. They are the world's only flight demonstration team to take off and land as a unit.

Chapter 4
The Snowbird Team

The Snowbird team includes 24 people. They are some of the most highly skilled members of the Canadian Forces.

Team Members
Snowbird members include 11 pilots, 10 maintenance technicians, and three support staff members. Snowbird pilots serve on the team for three years. Other team members serve for two years. The more experienced members train the new members.

Pilots, maintenance technicians, and support staff members make up the Snowbird team.

Duties

The Snowbird members perform various duties.
Nine pilots fly the aircraft in demonstrations.
The other two pilots are the coordinators. These
team members travel to each show. One
coordinator serves as a narrator by describing
the pilots' maneuvers to the audience. The other
coordinator matches music to the performances.
This team member also sometimes broadcasts
the pilots' communications to the audience. The
coordinators take turns performing these duties.

Ten aircraft technicians maintain and repair
the Tutors. These technicians make up the
ground crew.

The other three Snowbird members are a
logistics officer, a supply technician, and
a secretary. The logistics officer performs
administrative duties. These duties include
handling promotional materials and the
team's budget.

The supply technician makes sure enough
supplies are available. For example, this team
member makes sure the pilots have spare
airplane parts, oil, and brochures at shows.

**Technicians often check the Snowbirds' Tutors to
make sure they are working properly.**

Snowbird pilot candidates are mainly judged on their ability to fly in formation.

The secretary serves as an assistant to the logistics officer. The secretary is the only Snowbird member who is not in the military. There is no limit to the amount of time the secretary can serve on the team.

Becoming a Snowbird Pilot

Canadian Forces members who want to become Snowbird pilots must meet certain requirements. They must have at least 1,300 hours of military jet experience. Commanding officers in the Canadian Forces recommend pilots for the Snowbirds. The Snowbirds then invite six of these candidates to demonstrate their flying abilities at 15 Wing. The candidates stay at the base for about seven weeks.

The current Snowbird pilots choose the new pilots. The pilots are mainly chosen for their ability to fly in formation. The current pilots also consider each candidate's personality. All current pilots must agree on each choice.

The previous Snowbird boss and Air Force officials select the new boss. This pilot must have previously flown on

The Snowbirds practice flying near mountains in British Columbia.

the Snowbird team and hold the rank of major. This rank is above a captain and below a lieutenant colonel.

Only men have served as Snowbird pilots. Several women have tried to become pilots for the team. Women pilots may be part of the Snowbird team in the future.

Becoming a Snowbird Technician

Snowbird technicians need to have experience working on CT-114 Tutors. Commanding officers recommend technicians for the Snowbirds. The boss and crew chief then choose skilled candidates with excellent performance records. The crew chief supervises the ground crew.

The technicians fly with the Snowbird pilots to each air show. They make sure the planes are operating properly. The Snowbirds have never missed a show due to a plane's mechanical problems.

Pilot Training

The Snowbird pilots train at 15 Wing during winter and spring. They usually fly twice each day. The pilots fly only a few aircraft in formation at the beginning of training season. They gradually add more planes until all nine pilots are flying. The Snowbirds start with simple maneuvers. They practice until they can perform more difficult maneuvers. Each year, the Snowbird pilots complete about 200 training flights.

Each April, the Snowbirds spend three weeks flying near Comox, British Columbia, Canada. Part of the Rocky Mountains is located in British Columbia. The Snowbird pilots practice flying maneuvers near mountains. It is more difficult to fly in mountainous areas because there is no visible horizon. The pilots need to rely more on their planes' instruments to find out their locations.

Pilot Safety

Snowbird pilots wear safety equipment. They wear helmets that include a microphone, earphones, an oxygen system, and a visor. The microphone and earphones allow the pilots to communicate with one another. The oxygen system allows the pilots to breathe at high altitudes. The air at these heights contains little

The Snowbirds use helmets that contain an oxygen system.

oxygen. Visors help protect pilots' faces if an accident occurs.

Pilots sit in an ejection seat. Pilots use ejection seats if their planes are going to crash. The pilots pull a handle that shoots the ejection seat out of the plane. Ejection seats contain a parachute. These strong, lightweight pieces of fabric allow pilots to land safely on the ground or in water. The parachute opens when the seat falls away.

Snowbird pilots wear life vests when they fly over water. The life vests keep the pilots afloat if they land in water after an ejection.

Teaching Others

The Snowbirds sometimes speak to students at schools. They talk to the students about their duties as Snowbird pilots. They also encourage students to stay in school and avoid taking drugs.

The Snowbirds are representatives for a program called SMARTRISK. This program teaches young people how to prevent injuries. It encourages youth to wear seat belts, wear safety gear during sports, and take first aid classes. Snowbirds often promote this program when they speak to students.

The Snowbirds follow safety measures as they fly. They also teach others about safety.

Chapter 5
The Future

The Snowbirds are an important part of the Canadian Forces. They have many fans worldwide. But the future of the Snowbirds is uncertain.

Financial Problems
In September 1999, the Canadian government announced that it may not supply money for the Snowbirds to continue flying.

Throughout North America, fans of the Snowbirds wanted to save the team. They organized a project called "Save Our Snowbirds." They wrote postcards to members

It is uncertain how long the Snowbirds will continue to fly.

The Snowbirds will fly Tutors until 2006 if funding for the team continues.

of the Canadian government praising the
Snowbirds. In April 2000, the government
included money in its budget to continue the
Snowbirds until 2002. Officials also decided
that the Snowbirds would fly Tutors until 2006
if team funding continues.

New Planes

In 2000, pilots at 15 Wing began to fly training planes called Harvard IIs and Hawk 115s instead of Tutors. The Snowbirds then had less support from the base. In the past, other experienced Tutor pilots and technicians at 15 Wing provided support to the team.

The Canadian Air Force is considering having the Snowbirds fly other planes in the future. These planes include Harvard IIs or Hawk 115s.

The Snowbirds plan to enlarge their team due to the decreased support from 15 Wing. About 70 members soon will be part of the Snowbirds. Most of these team members will be technicians. Snowbird members who do not travel to shows also may serve longer terms.

The Snowbirds demonstrate the Canadian Forces' skill and teamwork to the North American public. People who respect and admire the team hope that they will perform for many more years.

Words to Know

aerobatics (air-uh-BAT-iks)—flying feats and maneuvers; pilots who do aerobatics perform rolls, loops, and dives.

biplane (BYE-plane)—an airplane with two sets of wings; biplanes usually have one wing located above the other.

cockpit (KOK-pit)—the area in a plane where the pilot sits

disband (diss-BAND)—to break up a unit in a military organization

maneuver (muh-NOO-ver)—a planned and controlled movement; pilots perform a series of maneuvers at air shows.

narrate (NA-rate)—to describe in detail

squadron (SKWAHD-ruhn)—an official military unit

throttle (THROT-uhl)—a valve in a vehicle's engine that opens to let steam, fuel, or fuel and air flow into it; the throttle controls a vehicle's speed.

To Learn More

Chant, Christopher. *Early Fighters.* The World's Greatest Aircraft. Philadelphia: Chelsea House, 1999.

Hopkins, Ellen. *The Thunderbirds: The U.S. Air Force Aerial Demonstration Squadron.* Serving Your Country. Mankato, Minn.: Capstone High-Interest Books, 2001.

Suen, Anastasia. *Air Show.* New York: Henry Holt, 2001.

Van Steenwyk, Elizabeth. *Air Shows: From Barnstormers to Blue Angels.* A First Book. New York: Franklin Watts, 1998.

Useful Addresses

Canadian Warplane Heritage Museum
Hamilton Airport
9280 Airport Road
Mount Hope, ON L0R 1W0
Canada

International Council of Air Shows
751 Miller Drive SE
Suite F-4
Leesburg, VA 20175

The Snowbirds
431 (AD) Sqn–Snowbirds
15 Wing
P.O. Box 5000
Moose Jaw, SK S6H 7Z8
Canada

Internet Sites

The Air Show Network
http://airshownetwork.com/home.html

Canada's Air Force
http://www.airforce.dnd.ca/airforce

Canadian Museum of Flight
http://www.canadianflight.org/index01.htm

15 Wing Moose Jaw
http://www.moosejaw.dnd.ca

431 (AD) Squadron Snowbirds
http://www.snowbirds.dnd.ca/index.asp

Index